Fasting: The Sleeping Giant
A Lost Discipline

Apostle Dr. Janice Owens

DEDICATION

I dedicate this book to
my husband, Charles Owens and
my three wonderful sons: Ron Toliver,
Guy Owens, and Blake Owens.

CONTENTS

ACKNOWLEDGMENTS

Pastor Janice Holman is a longtime friend and co-laborer and confidant of the ministry. We have traveled the nations together and have endured a lot together on the mission field. She has stood by my side as an encourager, a great teacher, and preacher of the Word of God. I am so grateful to have this opportunity to be graced with her awesome gift as an editor and publisher of this book.

Thank you Pastor Janice for your love and friendship.

INTRODUCTION

At this point in my life, I've been off the mission field and have established a ministry in our local area, and have been in much prayer. The Lord begin to remind me of a fasted lifestyle. Early in my walk, I fasted often to the point where people were concerned about my weight. He reminded me of the many miracles that I had experienced during the early years of my life, and all that happened as a result of living a fasting lifestyle. During the early time in my life, we were having numerous prayer meetings and gatherings. People were crying out to God for healing and deliverance in many areas with all their heart, yet weren't seeing many results. We would get the same desperate prayer requests week after week. and year after year. I needed to see the manifested power of God. We were getting discouraged and had a great concern for the people, and as we were seeking the Lord, I heard the Lord say that 'fasting was a lost art among many believers, including myself, and that some things don't come out except by fasting and praying'.

Mark 9:17-29 (NKJV) says:

17 Then one of the crowd answered and said, "Teacher, I brought You my son, who has a mute spirit. 18 And wherever it seizes him, it throws him down; he foams at the mouth, gnashes his teeth, and becomes rigid. So I spoke to Your disciples, that they should cast it out, but they could not." 19 He answered him and said, "O faithless generation, how long shall I be with you? How long shall I bear with you? Bring him to Me." 20 Then they brought him to Him. And when he saw Him, immediately the spirit convulsed him, and he fell on the ground and wallowed, foaming at the mouth. 21 So He asked his father, "How long has this been happening to him?" And he said, "From childhood. 22

And often he has thrown him both into the fire and into the water to destroy him. But if You can do anything, have compassion on us and help us." 23 Jesus said to him, "If you can believe, all things are possible to him who believes." 24 Immediately the father of the child cried out and said with tears, "Lord, I believe; help my unbelief!" 25 When Jesus saw that the people came running together, He rebuked the unclean spirit, saying to it, "Deaf and dumb spirit, I command you, come out of him and enter him no more!" 26 Then the spirit cried out, convulsed him greatly, and came out of him. And he became as one dead, so that many said, "He is dead." 27 But Jesus took him by the hand and lifted him up, and he arose. 28 And when He had come into the house, His disciples asked Him privately, "Why could we not cast it out?" 29 So He said to them, "This kind can come out by nothing but prayer and fasting."

God also reminded me of how Daniel and the Hebrew boys lived a fasted lifestyle and were found 10 times better than the others.

Daniel 1:12-21 (NKJV)

12 "Please test your servants for ten days: Give

us nothing but vegetables to eat and water to drink. 13 Then compare our appearance with that of the young men who eat the royal food, and treat your servants in accordance with what you see." 14 So he agreed to this and tested them for ten days. 15 At the end of the ten days they looked healthier and better nourished than any of the young men who ate the royal food. 16 So the guard took away their choice food and the wine they were to drink and gave them vegetables instead. 17 To these four young men God gave knowledge and understanding of all kinds of literature and learning. And Daniel could understand visions and dreams of all kinds. 18 At the end of the time set by the king to bring them into his service, the chief official presented them to Nebuchadnezzar. 19 The king talked with them, and he found none equal to Daniel, Hananiah, Mishael and Azariah; so they entered the king's service. 20 In every matter of wisdom and understanding about which the king questioned them, he found them ten times better than all the magicians and enchanters in his whole kingdom. 21 And Daniel remained there until the first year of King Cyrus.

A LIFESTYLE OF FASTING

When you read the Bible, you'll see how often they fasted. There were kings that fasted when they were in great danger and when they saw the enemy coming. Jehoshophat saw the enemy coming. The word of God told them there was way more than they could handle in their own strength. The Bible says that one day someone came to King Jehoshophat and warned him that a gigantic army was headed his way, determined to destroy them. It was hopeless. He went on a fast, and put all of Judah on a fast, and they came together and prayed. God gave them a great victory. Remember Jonah was sent to Nineveh. God told him to tell that great city that they were going to be destroyed in forty days. The Lord came in with a word of judgement. After Jonah finally obeyed the Lord and told the people of Nineveh, the King put everyone on a fast. Glory to God. Even the animals were put on a fast. God saw what they had done. The Bible says they fasted and cried mightily unto the Lord, and because they fasted and prayed, God changed his mind and did not destroy them like he had previously said. We can call on God. Sometimes God will send a word of judgement, and we know when he is speaking to us. When we are in a place where we sincerely seek him with our heart, with fasting and praying, God will show us mercy. He is a merciful God. He is gracious. He is full of compassion. I am reminded of the woman Anna, who was in the temple. The Bible says she fasted and prayed day and night. She was constantly fasting and praying. In the book of Esther, the Jews were about to be destroyed, because that wicked Hamen was out to destroy them. However, Esther called for a three day fast, and as a result God spared them (Esther 4:3,16; 9:31 NKJV).

Fasting is the sleeping giant because the flesh does not want to fast, to not eat, but there are benefits to fasting. We, the people of God, should take heed to the word of God. Jesus even told his disciples, when they couldn't cast the demon out of the boy, that some of these things do not come out, except by fasting and praying. So, there are times when we need to fast. Jesus even taught us how to fast. When you fast, do not look pitiful and the heavenly father who sees, will reward you openly (Matthew 6:16-18 NKJV). There were people who fasted forty days. Jesus fasted for forty days. Elijah, the prophet, fasted forty days. Moses fasted forty days. Glory to God. There are benefits to fasting. Nowadays, we get so many prayer requests. Yes, God hears and answers our prayers. When we take our prayers to God and we ask God to heal our loved ones, or deliver our rebellious children, or save our marriages, and with all our praying, we don't see anything, it may require us to pray and fast in that situation. We pray, we pray and we pray, but sometimes, it requires prayer and fasting. The enemy is operating in the world to hinder and prevent souls from being saved.

The devil is trying to come in and destroy God's

people. He has been attacking marriages. It's a demonic attack. We cannot be passive. Passive, meaning like, "Father deliver my husband, save my children"—no you must mean business when it comes to this devil. Some of these things do not come out without us sacrificing some meals. Because whether we want to acknowledge it or not, many times it's demonic activity that's at work. We must see it for what it is. It is demonic activity. The devil has launched a demonic attack against us and our families, so we must do what we need to do. We've got to take drastic measures sometimes and put that plate aside. I hear stuff like, "well I'm on medication", but you can go on a Daniel fast. You can still eat on a Daniel fast. You can still have fruits, vegetables, wheat, and water. So, there's no excuse. See the enemy wants to keep us from fasting because he knows the power behind fasting. I've found in ministry that fasting is very effective and causes the anointing to increase as you deny yourself. Many people are delivered and set free as a result of the fast (Mark 9:17-29).

When I was coming up in church, back in the day,

there were people who loved God and saw the glory of God. They fasted, and they saw the manifested power of God as a result of the fast. They saw strong deliverance take place in the lives of their loved ones, as a result of the fast. So, when God tells us to fast, we want to make sure we fast. Sometimes we must be like Jehoshophat, who set himself to seek the Lord with fasting and praying. When he understood the seriousness of the situation, he made a conscious decision that he would fast and pray, because he needed to hear from God. Same thing with Esther, the spirit of God did not lead her, or maybe so, but nonetheless, she decided to fast and pray because they needed a miracle from God. The account didn't even mention God, but we know that the Jews were God's chosen people. They knew about the Lord. They knew about God. There was a lot of fasting and praying that took place in the Old Testament, as well as the New Testament.

Fasting is the sleeping giant because it's a devil killer. I know what I'm talking about. I'll share a brief testimony with you. One of my sons had gotten in a lot of trouble, a lot of problems. I was a young woman, and I had just gotten saved. The devil was trying to kill my boy; he was trying to wipe him off the face of the earth. God put me on a consecration. I didn't know I could go on a consecration for that length of time. I was on a six-month consecration. It wasn't that I didn't eat, God just wouldn't allow me to eat breakfast for six months—a hundred and eighty days. I didn't realize he was going to do a 180 degree turn around for my son, but he did, praise God. I was fasting and praying because they were trying to give my son over thirty years in prison. They were working that thing. The way they had it positioned, they had every right. It was looking bad for him. Sometimes, some of these systems will have your loved ones looking as bad as they possibly can, because they are trying to make something stick. Some of that stuff will cause life in prison, but God, during that time of consecration, he anointed my eyes, my hands, my mouth and my feet. Things were being birthed in the realm of the spirit, even before I knew about travailing in the spirit. As a result of that fast, they dropped the charges on my son.

Praise God. It was a miracle.

God is the same God. He is not a different God. The God that worked in the Old Testament, is not a different God, or a different being. He is the same. The Bible says that Jesus is the same yesterday, today and forever more (Hebrews 13:8 NKJV). Read the entire chapter on fasting in Isaiah 58, and just take your time, it's very powerful. God's chosen fast. This is a time where wickedness has increased. The Bible talked about perilous and difficult times coming. We know and can see there's an operation of the devil even through our television sets. The conversations that we hear and all that's taking place. The enemy has raised his hand up, even against the people of God, by the laws that have been passed in the land. The Bible says that evil men would get worse and worse. We must be prepared. We can't be lukewarm. I praise God for this time of the year; it's a beautiful time. It's a joyous time of year. I am a person of celebration. I love to celebrate, especially when it comes to celebrating the goodness of God. David said that I had fainted unless I have believed and seen the goodness of God in the land of the living.

We have the ability as the saints of God. The Bible says if my people that are called by my name would humble themselves and pray and seek my face, and turn from their wicked ways, that he would hear from heaven. He would heal our land and forgive our sins—He is talking about the people of God (2 Chronicles 7:14). The world and its system; the stuff that's in the world is just going to be, but we have been translated out of the kingdom of darkness and into the kingdom of his dear son (Colossians 1:13). We are kingdom citizens. We have benefits; we have power. Jesus gave us power. Jesus gave power to his church, and when things don't seem to be happening like we expect, that's when we must take drastic measures. That's when we need to fast and pray. In the past, the people of God would fast once every week. The church leaders back then would say, "I'm scared of you because if you can't put the plate aside, if you can't deny your flesh, then I'm wondering if you can resist temptation; if you can resist sin. If you don't have strength or your flesh under control enough to where you can push the plate aside, where you can skip a meal, I wonder if you can resist temptation. I wonder if you can tell the devil no."

Daniel fasted twenty-one days (Daniel 10). Esther, she fasted three days. In the book of Jonah, the king and the people of Nineveh fasted three days. The Bible speaks about three-day fasts, forty-day fasts, and twenty-one-day fasts. We are the church of Jesus Christ and we live out of the Spirit of God. Whatever God tells you to do, do it, because it's for a reason.

If God tells you to fast, you want to obey the spirit of God, because it's for a serious reason. Many times, it may be a life and death situation. I know we don't like hearing this kind of stuff, but it's just the truth. I almost lost one of my sons—my middle son. When we were in California, I was invited one morning to go to this prayer breakfast with my friend, who used to travel with me. She had set up this beautiful prayer breakfast early one morning, and the anointed people of God had gathered. She had the tables laid; she knew how to set a table. Everything was beautiful, and everything that my heart desired was on that table. As I was getting ready to get my food, I heard the spirit of God say, "don't eat." I was like don't eat, in front of all these people? What is that going to look like? See you can't be worried about other folks. When God tells you to fast, you fast. I obeyed the spirit of God, even though my flesh wanted to eat very badly. I love strawberries, and they had strawberries on the table. She had everything, but the Lord said don't eat. I obeyed the Lord not knowing that my son, who is a musician, was on his way from Santa Barbara. I didn't even know he was out of town, but I just obeyed the Lord. My son was involved in a terrible car accident, and the car that he was in flipped over, and rolled a few times over the hill. It was a terrible car wreck, but God spared my son's life. There was another boy in the car, and my heart goes out to him and his family, but he didn't make it. God spared my son. I pray that God would use him for His glory, because his life was spared for a purpose. Praise God! So many times, we don't know who is interceding for us, or praying for us.

When I went to Florida, earlier this year, I had a friend from Africa who called me up three nights straight and prayed for me. God will raise up people. People that you least expect. He will raise them up to pray and make intercession for you. Often, they are praying and praying in secret. My friend would start praying in the Holy Ghost. It's good to pray in the Holy Ghost. Many times, when you don't know how to pray and don't know what you're praying about, you can sense the Spirit of God praying through you, don't hold it back (Romans 8:26). Yield your vessel and yield your temple, and allow the Spirit of God to make intercession through you. Somebody's life could be at stake. My life was at stake, because that devil tried to kill me. I had a horrible fall, but God spared me. I know he spared my life because it was a hard hit on my head, but my friend was interceding for me, and she didn't even know why she was calling me. I know she didn't know what she was praying about, but nonetheless, I know that this woman was making intercession for me, by the Spirit of the living God. Oftentimes, people don't understand the power of prayer. Prayer and intercession. Intercession means you're standing in for somebody, and many times, it requires fasting and praying. Sometimes you might be fasting for the nation, but you don't even know it. You just obey the

Spirit of God. If God tells you to fast, fast. Somebody's life could be at stake. You are the chosen vessel that he chose for that hour to use and intercede on behalf of somebody.

I'm reminded of Ezekiel where he said, "I look for a man." God was looking for somebody that would stand in the gap. Sometimes I wonder about people, because they are looking for something bad to happen to folks. He looked for a man. He is looking for people that would stand in behalf of the nation, so it wouldn't be destroyed. The Bible says God is merciful and He is gracious. The devil is the one who comes to steal, kill, and destroy. So, don't get it mixed up. Jesus said, "I come so that you might have life, and that they might have it more abundantly" (John 10:10 NKJV). The word of God tells us it's not the will of God that any man should perish, but that all should come to the knowledge of the truth. It is the will of God for you to be saved. It's his will for you. If you ever wonder about the will of God for your life, know that it's his will for you to live. He said I come, so you might have life, and have it more abundantly. Hallelujah. He tells us in

Timothy to pray for all men. Make intercession for all men—for kings and authority, even though we might not like them. The Bible says that God causes his sun to shine on the good and the evil. He causes the rain to fall on the good and the evil.

In the New Testament, the book of Acts (13:2-4) says, while they were worshipping the Lord and fasting. The Holy Ghost said set apart for me Barnabas and Saul for the work to which I have called them to. Notice it says, "after they had fasted"—they weren't just releasing people in ministry. They fasted first and prayed. They weren't just trying to get members or trying to get an extra dollar. They fasted and they prayed. They worshipped God. So, after they fasted and prayed, they placed their hands on them and sent them off. The two of them who were sent on their way by the Holy Ghost went down to Seleucia and sailed from there to Cyprus. There was much time spent with the Lord in prayer and fasting. That's why we shouldn't take these things lightly. Also, in Acts 14:23, the word of God says that Paul and Barnabas appointed elders in each church, and with prayer and fasting committed them to the Lord, in whom they have put their trust. Fast and pray for direction and for clarity. Fasting helps us to hear from God.

I was praying and fasting, and asking the Lord about what changes to make for the new year, and immediately after the prayer, one of my favorite apostles gave a prophetic word from the Lord. He said that you don't need something new. Everybody wants a new plan; a new word. He said just be consistent with what God has already given you. Praise God. That was the word. Be consistent, be faithful, and be dedicated to what God has already committed to you. The Bible says that a faithful man shall abound with blessings. The Lord heard me. He always hears me. Sometimes He tells you no, or maybe He has something better for you. God hears us and answers our prayers. He is a prayer answering God. As the people of God, the sold-out ones for the gospel of Jesus Christ, every born-again believer, have access to the throne of grace. We can obtain mercy and find help in time of need. What a mighty God we serve.

I got this in my spirit—that sometimes we don't

realize that we are picking up somebody's else's issues, symptoms, or feelings when we begin feeling sad or have a heavy heart. It's not always about us. Sometimes we might be picking up something else that we need to intercede or stand in the gap for, so we pray until the burden lifts. We could be the vessel that God is using, to intercede for that person that might be ready to commit suicide, or for someone who might feel like they can't make it for whatever reason, but God has moved and put the spirit of intercession upon us to stand in the gap. Sometimes He might put us on a fast, and we might not even know what we're fasting and praying for. Somebody's life could be at stake. We must obey the Spirit of God. We are spiritual beings, and the Spirit of God dwells on the inside of us. Praise God! He is using us. We are his vessels. We're carriers of his presence. We are carriers of his glory.

I think it's important that we make praying and fasting a lifestyle. We don't want to wait until there is an emergency before we pray or go on a three-day fast, or whatever. The Bible says that when Jesus came out of the wilderness after a forty-day fast, that is when his ministry took off. There is power in fasting. We must wake up that sleeping giant. It's a powerful tool that God has given to his people. If you have been praying for years and years for loved ones to be saved, and they aren't saved yet, how about adding some fasting? Fast for a day or two, for that individual, for their soul to be saved. It is important. Those that went to the doctor and was told all negative stuff, we don't have to just lay down and take it, we can fast. I'm telling you God will speak to you, when you really mean it. Also, we don't have to go around telling everybody that we're on a fast, and how long we've been fasting, and telling them that we're barely making it. We don't need to do that. The fast is unto God. Let it be in secret, and our Heavenly Father who sees in secret, will reward you openly. We need the power of God in our churches. We need the glory of God in our churches. Wake up that sleeping giant among the people of God. It is time to wake it up. Spend some time in fasting and prayer.

TESTIMONIES

How can fasting help believers? Fasting and prayer can help us hear from God, strengthen intimacy with God, and build our faith.

These testimonies provide examples of how God uses fasting to His glory.

Fasting Brings Deliverance from Car Wreck

I was invited to a Prayer Breakfast, which I had been looking forward to for weeks. I made preparation to be at the breakfast and was hungry. The breakfast was a beautiful elegant setting with the choice foods available on the table, including my favorites, and I heard the Lord say, "Don't Eat."

I knew from previous experiences that it is always better to obey the Lord, so I didn't eat, as instructed. Soon afterwards, we received a call from our son who was hours away from home saying he was in a horrible car wreck. The driver fell asleep at the wheel and died, but God spared my son's life. Fasting was instrumental in my son's deliverance.

Fasting Brings A Release from Prison

As a young woman, I was what many would call a good church going woman that loved God and her family. My son somehow got caught up with the wrong type of friends. For the most part he seemed to be a decent young man, but without me knowing it, he was involved with the wrong kinds of friends. I get a phone call saying my son is on TV, on fugitive watch, on the run from the police. I couldn't believe what I was hearing, especially the part about armed and dangerous, which meant he could be shot and killed by the police. I was able to convince my son to turn himself in to the police, which he did.

They had a pretty good case against him. He looked very bad in the courtroom and was threatened with 30 years or more in prison. God put me on a consecrated fast for 180 days. During this consecration, which came through a dream, the Lord gave me instructions to not eat before noon each day. Basically, I was to skip breakfast, which was my favorite meal of the day. The fasting caused me to draw even closer to God. His Presence would get stronger and stronger.

There were times that the fasting and praying would be so good that I didn't want to eat, so I would go days and days without eating. As a result of this fast, I had some awesome encounters with the Lord. The ministry was birthed, and I received numerous impartations from the Lord. During this time as I prayed and fasted, the Lord saved my son while he was in prison, and he became a mighty instrument used of the Lord behind the prison wall. He also received the baptism of the Holy Ghost, behind the prison wall, and led many to Christ. God used him to bring unity among gang members, and they loved and respected him.

I needed an attorney for my son, but didn't have the funds so a court appointed attorney was given who would normally cost $100,000, which I didn't have, but this man took my son's case. My son was in jail for almost a year before he went to court, but we continued with the fast. While they chose the jury—we were fasting. Every day that we were in the courtroom—we were fasting. The fast was so effective that when the attorney would speak on behalf of my son, he sounded like he was ten feet tall, and it seemed like the court room would shake.

During the fast, the Lord showed me a vision of my son being translated out of the prison clothed in glistering white with a staff in his hand. We continued fasting and praying and on a Monday morning when we returned to the courthouse, we found the jury sitting outside the courtroom. I was told that the charges were dropped due to a technicality. After weeks and weeks of being in that courtroom, it was a miracle because based on the evidence he could've been in prison for most of His life, but God showed him mercy and he is now a great teacher and preacher of the 21st Century, and is impacting many lives.

Healing through the power of fasting and prayer

My husband was very sick for several years. It went from bad to worst. The doctors couldn't get his blood pressure down, and he was diagnosed with congestive heart failure. We were back and forth to the doctor every week. Then it got so bad that they had to give him oxygen in a container that had to be set up at home. During this time, I could hardly leave the house or go to sleep at night afraid that he would pull the tubes out of his nose, which he would often do. Sometimes it was so frightening I just didn't know what to do.

I've always been a person of prayer and intercession, which included fasting. Throughout this fiery trial, God would give me directions as to what to do and where to go concerning my husband. If I fell asleep, God would wake me up to be there for him, if needed. As we went back and forth to the hospitals, they would often misdiagnose him and God would use me to walk them through what he needed. On several occasions, he almost died and God used me to lay hands on him and practically raise him from the dead. When it looked like he wouldn't survive this whole ordeal, God would show up and show Himself strong on our behalf.

On one occasion, as I sought the Lord in prayer and fasting, God showed me in a quick vision which hospital to take him to, because we found that when we took him to a different hospital, they had to start over again with evaluating and trying to determine what was going on with him, which wasted precious time. I sought the Lord, and He showed me in a vision which hospital to take him to. As a result of this step of obedience, he was hospitalized and one thing led to another where he ended up in ICU and transported to a hospital that had all the necessary equipment and specialists, who were able to run the proper tests, and found out that he was being treated for the wrong type of blood pressure—for over 30 years. God spared his life as a result of fasting and praying.

Isaiah 58:7-9 (NKJV) states:

> 7 Is it not to share your food with the hungry and to provide the poor wanderer with shelter—when you see the naked, to clothe them, and not to turn away from your own flesh and blood?

> 8 Then your light will break forth like the dawn, and your healing will quickly appear; then your righteousness will go before you, and the glory of the Lord will be your rear guard.

> 9 Then you will call, and the Lord will answer; you will cry for help, and he will say: Here am I.

Receiving a new home through fasting and prayer

On one occasion, we were believing God for a house. God showed me in a dream where to look for a house. We looked at about 10 houses, and I prayed again asking God which house, and he showed me the roof of a house, which was the least out of all the houses we had looked at. We went through the loan process, but it didn't go through because at that time I was working as a contractor and they couldn't use my employment because I needed a permanent job. The realtor told me that if I could get a job in the same field that they would be able to use my previous years of employment to qualify for the house. It really shook me up because I knew beyond a doubt that the Lord had said that this was our house. So, I applied for a job at Southwest Airlines. Although there were over 300 applicants for the job, they hired me. During the interview, the interviewer said that as I would talk my face would light up, which was the result of fasting and praying.

I had to go to Dallas for training. The class was full of young adults, but nevertheless through much prayer and fasting, and because my mind was keen through fasting and praying, I was able to pass the class—and was almost valedictorian. After passing the class and working in a high stress environment, by the grace of God, we were able to finally qualify for that house making the least amount of money that I ever worked for. I had to work for three months before I was considered permanent, but through much prayer and fasting, I was able to learn the various systems and found much favor with the people. God blessed us with that house that He showed me in the dream, which eventually led to our dream home.

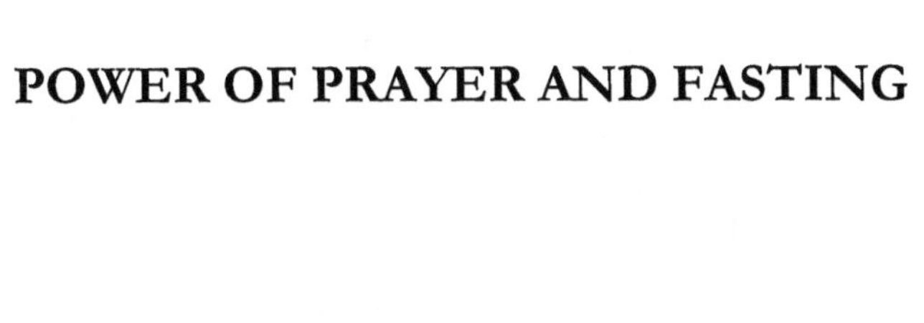

POWER OF PRAYER AND FASTING

Prayer and fasting can change any situation.

Job Situation

As a wife, mother, grandmother and intercessor, it requires a lifestyle of praying and fasting. On many occasions, due to much opposition in the workplace, it required fasting and praying. On one occasion, my coworker and I were working in a department that was extremely hostile. We were under constant threat of losing our jobs. We would fast and pray, by often skipping lunch, and we would take prayer walks. We watched God remove the wicked people, who were constantly plotting against us, although we hadn't done them any harm. There was a new hire, who thought that he had special favor with the leadership. He would go in and out of the manager's office constantly complaining about us. So, we always felt threatened by him.

We continued to fast and pray, and one night I had a dream of a picture of him hanging on a clothes line. He was caught doing something devious, and they fired him. The jobs that we had were contract jobs, so they weren't considered permanent positions. Although we had been doing the job for over two years, new positions had to be created that would make the positions permanent, which required them to post the jobs before offering us the position. We continued fasting and praying, and the vice president of the company told them to remove the postings and to give us those jobs.

On another occasion, I had accepted an invitation to Africa at Christmas time and requested the time off in January, just to make sure there wouldn't be any problems getting the time off, but they denied me the time anyway. But I heard the Lord say don't cancel your plans to Africa. As time went on, we continued with the fasting and praying due to the hostile environment. A few months later we received a companywide email stating that the entire company would be shut down for two weeks during Christmas time, which meant although the management wouldn't grant me the time off, the time was granted by a Higher Power, and I was able to continue with my plans. This company hadn't had a shut down in over 30 years. As we continued fasting and praying, the Lord cleaned the environment up and the whole department was swept clean. All the wicked people were let go or moved on for other reasons. Leading a lifestyle of fasting and praying caused me to be granted much favor with God and man.

Marriage

In the past, the enemy was working overtime to destroy my marriage, but through much fasting and praying the Lord would grant many breakthroughs and my husband and I have managed to stay together for over 35 years.

Promotions at the Job

Many times, I had to take exams to qualify for promotions, and I would often fast and pray and the positions were granted, although I didn't qualify on paper. Sometimes after a test, they would ask me questions on how I studied for the test to know how I was able to do so well. I know it had a lot to do with fasting and praying.

Daniel 1:3-8, 15-17, 20 (NKJV) says:

3 And the king spake unto Ashpenaz the master of his eunuchs, that he should bring certain of

the children of Israel, and of the king's seed, and of the princes;

4 Children in whom was no blemish, but well favoured, and skilful in all wisdom, and cunning in knowledge, and understanding science, and such as had ability in them to stand in the king's palace, and whom they might teach the learning and the tongue of the Chaldeans.

5 And the king appointed them a daily provision of the king's meat, and of the wine which he drank: so nourishing them three years, that at the end thereof they might stand before the king.

6 Now among these were of the children of Judah, Daniel, Hananiah, Mishael, and Azariah:

7 Unto whom the prince of the eunuchs gave names: for he gave unto Daniel the name of Belteshazzar; and to Hananiah, of Shadrach; and to Mishael, of Meshach; and to Azariah, of Abednego.

8 But Daniel purposed in his heart that he would not defile himself with the portion of the king's meat, nor with the wine which he drank:

therefore he requested of the prince of the eunuchs that he might not defile himself.

15 And at the end of ten days their countenances appeared fairer and fatter in flesh than all the children which did eat the portion of the king's meat.

16 Thus Melzar took away the portion of their meat, and the wine that they should drink; and gave them pulse.

17 As for these four children, God gave them knowledge and skill in all learning and wisdom: and Daniel had understanding in all visions and dreams.

20 And in all matters of wisdom and understanding, that the king enquired of them, he found them ten times better than all the magicians and astrologers that were in all his realm.

TYPES OF BIBLICAL FASTING

- **A Regular Fast** - Traditionally, a regular fast means refraining from eating all food. Most people still drink water or juice during a regular fast. When Jesus fasted in the desert, the Bible says, "After fasting forty days and forty nights, he was hungry." This verse does not mention Jesus being thirsty.

- **A Partial Fast** - This type of fast generally refers to omitting a specific meal from your diet or refraining from certain types of foods. Daniel 10:2-3 says, "At that time I, Daniel, mourned for three weeks. I ate no choice food; no meat or wine touched my lips; and I used no lotions at all until the three weeks were over." In Daniel 1:12, they restricted their diet to vegetables and water: "Please test your servants for ten days: Give us nothing but vegetables to eat and water to drink."

- **A Full Fast** - These fasts are complete - no food and no drink. Acts 9:9 describes when Paul went on a full fast for three days following his encounter with Jesus on the road to Damascus: "For three days he was blind, and did not eat or drink anything."

Esther also called for this type of fast in Esther 4:15-16: "Then Esther sent this reply to Mordecai: 'Go, gather together all the Jews who are in Susa, and fast for me. Do not eat or drink for three days, night or day. I and my maids will fast as you do. When this is done, I will go to the king, even though it is against the law. And if I perish, I perish.'" It is recommended that this type of fast be done with extreme caution and not for extended periods of time.

- **A Sexual Fast** - 1 Corinthians 7:3-6 says, "The husband should fulfill his marital duty to his wife, and likewise the wife to her husband. The wife's body does not belong to her alone but also to her husband. In the same way, the husband's body does not belong to him alone but also to his wife. Do not deprive each other except by mutual consent and for a time, so that you may devote yourselves to prayer. Then come together again so that Satan will not tempt you because of your lack of self-control."

Today, Christians commit to fasting from other activities as well. These are not mentioned in the Bible.

Some give up entertainment, such as TV or movies to concentrate on prayer. Others fast from sleep or another activity for a specified period.

KEY TIMES OF FASTING

You'll see that there are many different reasons to fast and many examples in the Bible about fasting. Within the following examples, there are variations on what the fast included.

Moses Fasted Before Receiving the Commandments – Deuteronomy 9:9-18

Moses fasted during the 40 days and 40 nights when he was on the mountain receiving the law from God. Moses says that he did not eat food nor drink water during the 40 days (Deuteronomy 9:9). *Remember that a human body cannot survive extended periods of time without water unless God works a miracle.*

After he came down from the mountain of God and saw the people in sin, Moses angrily breaks the tablets of stone. Later, he again goes to the mountain and fasts another 40 days without food and water before receiving the law once more (Deuteronomy 9:18, 25, 26; 10:10).

David Mourning His Child's Illness – 2 Samuel 12:1-23

After David had committed adultery with Bathsheba he learned that she was pregnant. David had her husband so he could have Bathsheba as his wife. After the baby was born, Nathan the prophet, confronted David about his sin. David confessed and repented (2 Samuel 12:1-14).

Even though David repented before God, there were still consequences for his actions. The prophet told David that the child would die. The child became very ill. David immediately went into prayer and fasting for his son. He knew that God said the child would die, but he had hoped that he might find grace in the eyes of God.

David refused to eat while the child was ill. After the seventh day his son died. When David found out about the child's death, he cleaned himself up, ceased from his mourning and began to eat once again (2 Samuel 12:15-20).

Elijah Fasted While Escaping Jezebel – 1 Kings 19:4-8
Wicked Queen Jezebel threatened to kill the prophet Elijah after he won the great victory over the prophets of Baal on Mount Carmel. Elijah fled to Beer-sheba then traveled another day into the wilderness.

Elijah found a juniper tree and rested. An angel came and fed him (1 Kings 19:5, 6). Elijah took the food and then went back to sleep. Elijah traveled for 40 days in the strength of that food until he arrived at Mount Horeb (1 Kings 19:7, 8). This is the same mountain where Moses received the Ten Commandments.

Ezra Fasted While Mourning Over Sin – Ezra 10:6-17
The Jews began to return to Israel after the Babylonian captivity. Ezra gathered the people together to confront them for their sins.

Ezra 10:6 does not say specifically how long his fast was (though there is indication that it lasted 3 days while waiting for the people to gather). The Bible does tell us that he did not eat any bread and only drank water during this fast. He fasted because he was mourning the sins of those who had been carried away from Israel, but had finally returned.

Esther Fasted for the Safety of the Jews – Esther 4:15-17
Mordecai heard that the Jews were to be exterminated from the kingdom of Ahasuerus. The reason for the genocide was because one man, Haman, did not like Mordecai and his family. He felt that Mordecai did not show him proper respect.

Queen Esther was a Jew, but Haman did not know

this. Mordecai came to his cousin Esther to ask her to petition the king to spare the Jews. Because of royal tradition, it was not appropriate for Esther to enter the king's court without an invitation. Even as queen she could be executed for approaching the king without an invitation (Esther 4:11).

Esther agreed to approach the king, but she asked Mordecai to spread the word to the Jews that they should fast for three days without food or drink. She fasted in the same manner.

Esther was accepted into the presence of the king and the Jewish people were saved.

Darius Fasted for Daniel's Safety – Daniel 6:18-23
Darius, the king of Persia, fasted all night after he was forced to put Daniel in the den of lions (Daniel 6:18). King Darius was tricked into signing a law that put his friend Daniel in grave danger. The punishment for this crime was to be cast into a den of lions.

Daniel was caught praying to God. He was brought before the king who had no ability to back out of the law even though Daniel was his friend. King Darius said that he hoped Daniel's God would be powerful enough to save Daniel from the lions.

Darius went to his home and fasted. The Bible does not say what this fast included, but it seems to indicate it was more than just food. We are told that the king did not allow music to be played that night, and he did not sleep. The king forfeited more than food for his fast.

In the morning, King Darius found that Daniel had survived the night. The king declared that God's power was greater than all the kingdoms of the earth. He proclaimed that God's kingdom would be established forever (Daniel 6:25-28).

Daniel Fasted for an Answer to Prayer – Daniel 10:1-3
Daniel fasted and prayed for understanding of a vision in Daniel 10. Verses 2 and 3 tell us that this fast was for three weeks. The vision Daniel saw showed what would become of the people of God in the future.

FASTING SCRIPTURES
(Scriptures are from the NIV)

Through many examples in the Bible, we can see and know that God grants supernatural revelation and wisdom through fasting. Fasting will help increase our intimacy with Christ and will open our eyes to what He wants to teach us.
If you are wondering how to fast, what to abstain from, and what to pray, these Bible verses about fasting will help guide you on your journey!

Both the Old Testament and New Testament teaches us the value of fasting, which is abstaining from food or drink in order to focus on prayer and seeking God's will.

NEW TESTAMENT FASTS

1 Corinthians 7:5

5 Do not deprive each other except perhaps by mutual consent and for a time, so that you may devote yourselves to prayer. Then come together again so that Satan will not tempt you because of your lack of self-control.

Acts 13:2

2 While they were worshiping the Lord and fasting, the Holy Spirit said, "Set apart for me Barnabas and Saul for the work to which I have called them."

Acts 14:23

23 Paul and Barnabas appointed elders for them

in each church and, with prayer and fasting, committed them to the Lord, in whom they had put their trust.

Luke 2:37

37 and then was a widow until she was eighty-four. She never left the temple but worshiped night and day, fasting and praying.

Luke 18:12

12 I fast twice a week and give a tenth of all I get.

Acts 13:3-4

3 So after they had fasted and prayed, they placed their hands on them and sent them off. 4 The two of them, sent on their way by the Holy Spirit, went down to Seleucia and sailed from there to Cyprus.

Matthew 6:16-18

16 "When you fast, do not look somber as the hypocrites do, for they disfigure their faces to show others they are fasting. Truly I tell you, they have received their reward in full. 17 But when you fast, put oil on your head and wash

your face, 18 so that it will not be obvious to others that you are fasting, but only to your Father, who is unseen; and your Father, who sees what is done in secret, will reward you."

Luke 4:2-4

2 where for forty days he was tempted by the devil. He ate nothing during those days, and at the end of them he was hungry. 3 The devil said to him, "If you are the Son of God, tell this stone to become bread." 4 Jesus answered, "It is written: 'Man shall not live on bread alone.'"

Luke 18:1-12

1 Then Jesus told his disciples a parable to show them that they should always pray and not give up. 2 He said: "In a certain town there was a judge who neither feared God nor cared what people thought. 3 And there was a widow in that town who kept coming to him with the plea, 'Grant me justice against my adversary.' 4 "For some time he refused. But finally he said to himself, 'Even though I don't fear God or care

what people think, 5 yet because this widow keeps bothering me, I will see that she gets justice, so that she won't eventually come and attack me!'" 6 And the Lord said, "Listen to what the unjust judge says. 7 And will not God bring about justice for his chosen ones, who cry out to him day and night? Will he keep putting them off? 8 I tell you, he will see that they get justice, and quickly. However, when the Son of Man comes, will he find faith on the earth?" 9 To some who were confident of their own righteousness and looked down on everyone else, Jesus told this parable: 10 "Two men went up to the temple to pray, one a Pharisee and the other a tax collector. 11 The Pharisee stood by himself and prayed: 'God, I thank you that I am not like other people—robbers, evildoers, adulterers—or even like this tax collector. 12 I fast twice a week and give a tenth of all I get.'"

OLD TESTAMENT FASTS

1 Samuel 7:7

7 When the Philistines heard that Israel had assembled at Mizpah, the rulers of the Philistines came up to attack them. When the Israelites heard of it, they were afraid because of the Philistines.

2 Samuel 1:12

12 They mourned and wept and fasted till evening for Saul and his son Jonathan, and for the army of the LORD and for the nation of Israel, because they had fallen by the sword.

Daniel 10:3

3 I ate no choice food; no meat or wine touched

my lips; and I used no lotions at all until the three weeks were over.

Esther 4:16

16 "Go, gather together all the Jews who are in Susa, and fast for me. Do not eat or drink for three days, night or day. I and my attendants will fast as you do. When this is done, I will go to the king, even though it is against the law. And if I perish, I perish."

Exodus 34:28

28 Moses was there with the LORD forty days and forty nights without eating bread or drinking water. And he wrote on the tablets the words of the covenant—the Ten Commandments.

Joel 2:12

12 "Even now," declares the LORD, "return to me with all your heart, with fasting and weeping and mourning."

Nehemiah 1:4

4 When I heard these things, I sat down and

wept. For some days I mourned and fasted and prayed before the God of heaven.

Psalm 69:10

10 When I weep and fast, I must endure scorn;

Psalm 35:13-14

13 Yet when they were ill, I put on sackcloth and humbled myself with fasting. When my prayers returned to me unanswered, 14 I went about mourning as though for my friend or brother. I bowed my head in grief as though weeping for my mother.

Joel 2:12-13

12 "Even now," declares the LORD, "return to me with all your heart, with fasting and weeping and mourning." 13 Rend your heart and not your garments. Return to the LORD your God, for he is gracious and compassionate, slow to anger and abounding in love, and he relents from sending calamity.

Daniel 9:3-5

3 So I turned to the Lord God and pleaded with him in prayer and petition, in fasting, and in sackcloth and ashes. 4 I prayed to the LORD my God and confessed: "Lord, the great and awesome God, who keeps his covenant of love with those who love him and keep his commandments, 5 we have sinned and done wrong. We have been wicked and have rebelled; we have turned away from your commands and laws."

2 Samuel 12:15-17

15 After Nathan had gone home, the LORD struck the child that Uriah's wife had borne to David, and he became ill. 16 David pleaded with God for the child. He fasted and spent the nights lying in sackcloth on the ground. 17 The elders of his household stood beside him to get him up from the ground, but he refused, and he would not eat any food with them.

1 Kings 21:25-27

25 (There was never anyone like Ahab, who sold

himself to do evil in the eyes of the LORD, urged on by Jezebel his wife. 26 He behaved in the vilest manner by going after idols, like the Amorites the LORD drove out before Israel.) 27 When Ahab heard these words, he tore his clothes, put on sackcloth and fasted. He lay in sackcloth and went around meekly.

Ezra 8:21-23

21 There, by the Ahava Canal, I proclaimed a fast, so that we might humble ourselves before our God and ask him for a safe journey for us and our children, with all our possessions. 22 I was ashamed to ask the king for soldiers and horsemen to protect us from enemies on the road, because we had told the king, "The gracious hand of our God is on everyone who looks to him, but his great anger is against all who forsake him." 23 So we fasted and petitioned our God about this, and he answered our prayer.

Isaiah 58:3-7

3 'Why have we fasted,' they say, 'and you have

not seen it? Why have we humbled ourselves, and you have not noticed?' "Yet on the day of your fasting, you do as you please and exploit all your workers. 4 Your fasting ends in quarreling and strife, and in striking each other with wicked fists. You cannot fast as you do today and expect your voice to be heard on high. 5 Is this the kind of fast I have chosen, only a day for people to humble themselves? Is it only for bowing one's head like a reed and for lying in sackcloth and ashes? Is that what you call a fast, a day acceptable to the LORD? 6 "Is not this the kind of fasting I have chosen: to loose the chains of injustice and untie the cords of the yoke, to set the oppressed free and break every yoke? 7 Is it not to share your food with the hungry and to provide the poor wanderer with shelter— when you see the naked, to clothe them, and not to turn away from your own flesh and blood?"

Jonah 3:5-9

5 The Ninevites believed God. A fast was proclaimed, and all of them, from the greatest to

the least, put on sackcloth. 6 When Jonah's warning reached the king of Nineveh, he rose from his throne, took off his royal robes, covered himself with sackcloth and sat down in the dust. 7 This is the proclamation he issued in Nineveh: "By the decree of the king and his nobles: Do not let people or animals, herds or flocks, taste anything; do not let them eat or drink. 8 But let people and animals be covered with sackcloth. Let everyone call urgently on God. Let them give up their evil ways and their violence. 9 Who knows? God may yet relent and with compassion turn from his fierce anger so that we will not perish."

ABOUT AUTHOR

Apostle Janice Owens became a born again, spirit-filled Christian at the age of 25. She has faithfully, without ceasing, served and labored in the ministry of the Lord for the past 30 years. She flows in the prophetic gift of the Spirit and the laying on of hands. A crucial part of her ministry consists of ministering to the poor, sick, and afflicted. Apostle Owen's message helps people find hope and restoration through Jesus Christ our Lord and Savior.

The Lord launched her into an extensive international ministry to England, Zimbabwe, Mozambique, Jamaica, the Kingdom of Swaziland, Zambia, Kenya, South Africa, Tanzania, and locally within the United States.

Today, she continues to pursue her passion for spreading the Gospel of Jesus Christ to distinguished world leaders, such as kings, queens, and prime ministers, as well as to the masses at home.

She holds an honorary Doctor of Divinity, in Religious Education from the Gospel Ministry Outreach Theology Institute, Houston, Texas.

Apostle Owens have been married to her supportive husband, Charles for over 30 years and they have three wonderful sons, Ron, Guy, and Blake. They also have three adorable grandchildren. She and Charles reside in Natchez, Mississippi, where she is currently teaching and preaching the unadulterated word of God.

Apostle Janice Owens is widely known as an Apostle of Faith.

Additional Book(s) by Apostle Janice Owens

THE KINGLY ANOINTING

For additional copies of this printed book
and to order the E-book Kindle version, go to
Amazon.com.

www.ingramcontent.com/pod-product-compliance
Lightning Source LLC
Chambersburg PA
CBHW061043050726

47592CB00004B/1569